WEST COUNTRY TOUR

Cover: St Michael's Mount

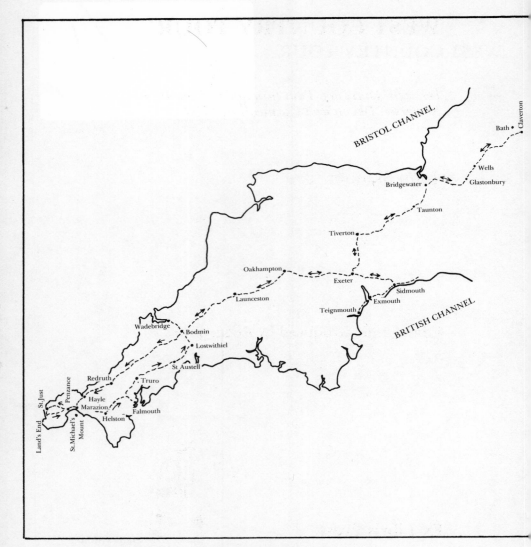

Map of the West of England showing John Skinner's route in 1797

WEST COUNTRY TOUR

*being the Diary of a Tour through the Counties of
Somerset, Devon and Cornwall in 1797*

John Skinner

Edited and introduced by Roger Jones

Ex Libris Press

First published in 1985 by
Ex Libris Press
1 The Shambles
Bradford on Avon
Wiltshire

Cover calligraphy by Peggy Cussins
Typeset in 9.5 on 11 point Baskerville
by Saxon Printing Ltd., Derby
Printed by A. Wheaton and Co., Ltd., Exeter

ISBN 0 9506563 9 9

Acknowledgements

John Skinner's *Diary* is from a manuscript from Somerset Archaeological Society's collection deposited in Somerset Record Office under reference DD/SAS C/1193/10; my thanks to Somerset County Archivist, Derek M.M.Shorrocks, for his assistance in pursuit of its publication here. My thanks are also due to Miss A.J.Shute, Devon County Librarian, for permission to use engravings from the West Country Studies Library and to Ian Maxted of W.C.S.L. for his help in arranging for copies to be made of the engravings reproduced. Others who have helped in the production of this book include David Hopkinson, who has helped greatly in the editing process (and even rewritten parts of the Introduction), Mr M.Thomas, Assistant County Librarian of East Cornwall for enlightenment on Cornish matters, R.S.Best of Marazion whose enthusiasm for the project greatly encouraged me, and Jean Darke who assisted with proof reading.

A Note on the Text

The original manuscript is in a small, neat, forward sloping hand which, although written nearly two centuries ago, is completely legible. The text, as reproduced here, represents about four fifths of the original. Nothing has been added, not even modern spellings in instances where these differ from Skinner's own; passages which have been omitted comprise those descriptive of places or history which lack any originality but have quite obviously been copied from existing guide books. All the footnotes have been added to clarify points in the text – Ed.

A Note on the
Illlustrations

I had always envisaged that *West Country Tour* should be accompanied by contemporary engravings. I was well acquainted with those which appeared in the series of books entitled *The Beauties of England and Wales,* compiled by John Britton and Edward Brayley, many volumes of which were published in the first half of the last century. A further series dealing with various counties, entitled *Views of ...,* also appeared but in a larger format and with more engravings. By the second quarter of the nineteenth century the vogue for finely illustrated topographical books was well established – there must have been a considerable demand for competent artists and engravers.

Most of the engravings here are from Britton and Brayley's *Views of Devon and Cornwall* (pages 37,40,42,44,52,57,65,73,77,80,86, and 88), others are from Rev. T. Moore's *History of Devonshire* (pages 24,26,29,31, and 35) and that on page 16 is from *Britton's Views of Bath and Bristol,* whilst the portrait of John Skinner of Page 13 is reproduced from the first edition of *Journal of a Somerset Rector* (John Murray, 1930). The engravings date from around 1830 which is, it must be admitted, a whole generation later than Skinner's tour, though still, significantly, a pre-Railway Age. The engravings in Britton and Brayley's *Views* series and those in Moore's book possess a quality and degree of realism which establishes them as far superior to those of an earlier period, which often tend to be generalised and idealised. Many of the same artists and engravers were employed to illustrate both Britton and Brayley's books and Moore's book: the use of those engravings here, I hope, lends a pleasing unity – Ed.

Introduction

Home tourism had been gaining in popularity throughout the eighteenth century when John Skinner undertook his West Country tour during two months in the autumn of 1797.

The close of the previous century witnessed the journeys of the intrepid Celia Fiennes, a lady who covered more or less the whole length of the country between 1685 and 1705. The vivid account of her travels was entitled *Through England on a Side Saddle in the Time of William and Mary* and was not published until 1888. Daniel Defoe published his *A Tour through the Whole Island of Great Britain* in the 1720s and this work is the product of several circuits made over previous years. Both writers set out to see and report on contemporary England and neither were especially interested in antiquities. They enthused over the cultivated countryside and scenes of industrial and commercial activity; wild and natural landscape generally left them unmoved.

At the same time that Daniel Defoe was enquiring into trade and manufacture up and down the country, William Stukely was searching for antiquities in every corner of the land. His passion was for the Roman and prehistoric – the hill forts and tumuli of Wessex especially attracted him. He was an archaeologist both scholarly and practical who conducted many tours from 1710 onwards. His observations and discoveries were published in his *Itinerarium*

Curiosum, or an *Account of the Antiquitys and Remarkable Curiositys in Nature or Art, Observ'd in Travels thro' Great Britain.*

Other absorbing interests of the eighteenth century tourist included visiting country houses and gardens. The thousands who now flock to National Trust properties, among other stately piles, are following in the footsteps of the tourists of two centuries ago, though this pastime was once confined to gentlemen and ladies of leisure.

The Reverend William Gilpin defined his theory of the picturesque in a series of works which he illustrated himself entitled *Observations;* these dealt with various parts of the country wherever wild and romantic scenery was apparent. *Observations of the River Wye* was published in 1770 and was followed by many others, including volumes dealing with the much favoured Lake District and North Wales. The disciples of Gilpin, and there were many, set out in search of the ideal landscape.

The new turnpike roads which began to multiply after the mid-eighteenth century meant that overland travel became less of a travail and a much more agreeable activity, though roads and inns in the farther flung parts of the country were often far from adequate. Certainly much of Devon and Cornwall fell into this category; John Skinner remarks upon the poor state of the roads, sometimes, as between Exeter and Okehampton, due to the incompetence of the road builders. He notices the state of the pavements in some of the towns he visits and comments on the improvements made at Truro since the Lighting and Paving Act if 1794.

It may seem a curious fact to us that for the Georgian tourist, the attraction of picturesque landscape was often accompanied by a fascination with all forms of industrial activity. The focus of attention in landscape was now not the richness and variety of English agriculture but rather the wild and romantic view of lake, mountain and crag.

The blast furnace, the mine and the factory drew the curious tourist who often accumulated considerable knowledge of the techniques and organisation of industry.

Oddly, too, prisons sometimes provided another place of interest for the Georgian tourist. John Howard, the indefatigable prison reformer, perhaps began this fashion with the publication, in 1777, of his account of contemporary prisons entitled *The State of Prisons in England and Wales, with an Account of some Foreign Prisons.* Skinner alludes to Howard's ideas after making a visit to Bodmin Gaol.

So it was that the extended tour around parts of England became a fashionable pursuit among the gentlemen and ladies of Georgian England. The Lake District and North Wales were the most popular destinations but almost all parts of the country were visited, including the Wye Valley, South Wales, Scotland, Durham and Northumberland, and the Peak District. The West Country, however, was not the magnet for tourists which it is today. The poor state of its roads and relative isolation was one reason; neither did it rate very highly, to one's surprise, in the league of picturesque landscape. New industries were not developing as vigorously here as in some parts of the country, although the Cornish metal mines were a considerable attraction, as was the romance of Devon and Cornwall's maritime connections.

The new fashion for home travel was followed by a multitude of accounts of travels undertaken. Many hundreds of such accounts were published but many more remain as manuscripts to this day. Some include lengthy descriptions of the guide book type, often copied word for word, and with little or no "human interest", or evidence of first hand observation. Others focus on the author's own particular interest: agricultural practice, geology, archaeology, or whatever.

The appeal of John Skinner's tour, presented here, is that it has a freshness and a vitality which reveals the enthusiasm and wide ranging curiosity of the young man who undertook this journey. He is aware of "the picturesque", and more than once sets down to sketch a picturesque view, but he is not as one-track-minded in this respect as many of his contemporaries. His predilection is for castles and earthworks, for industry such as the tin and copper mines of Cornwall and for fishing, with detailed accounts of salmon fishing in the Teign and Camel estuaries as well as the Cornish pilchard fishery. He is interested in history certainly, but he seems equally interested in the social and economic problems of his own time, especially perhaps on improvements to the public services. He is almost always keenly interested in the people he meets and the stories they tell him. He is naturally class concious, noting the ungentlemanlike appearance of certain naval officers in charge of French prisoners at Falmouth, but he is not in the least snobbish. It is the life of the common people that he wishes to observe and record.

His Christian conscience finds expression in his writing, notably in a feeling of outrage over General Kirk's cruelty following Monmouth's Rebellion and in his compassionate attitude to prisoners in Bodmin Gaol. He is less prejudiced against non-conformists than one might expect. On several occasions he records meeting with Quakers whom he liked and respected sometimes, it seems, to his own surprise. His general outlook is liberal, tolerant and free of sectarian jealousy. It seems to give him satisfaction that among the various sects in Penzance, all had a separate place of worship. He also records with pleasure and respect that the West Cornish miners usually attended Meeting before they came to church and ended their Sundays with prayers and exhortations in each other's houses.

-John Skinner was born in 1772 at Claverton, a village in the Avon valley a few miles upstream from Bath on the border of Somerset and Wiltshire. Claverton had been the home of Ralph Allen, whose vision and entrepreneurial flair lay behind the eighteenth century rebuilding of Bath. In his journey back through Cornwall, John Skinner went out of his way to find and sketch the humble cottage where Ralph Allen spent his younger days. Skinner went up to Oxford in 1797, the year in which he was ordained. In 1794 he went to Lincoln's Inn though he did not long pursue the profession of the Law.

The first leg of our narrator's journey through the south-western counties took him to Wells. He explored nearby Wookey Hole but spent the next three days preparing his Ordination Sermon. Having received his papers and been ordained, Skinner resumed his holiday tour and reached Sidmouth two days later, via Glastonbury, Bridgewater, Taunton, Tiverton and Exeter. Here he took lodgings for a month and, chancing to meet an acquaintance from Southampton, joined him in an excursion across the Exe estuary to Teignmouth. He spent his time at Sidmouth in riding out into the country and along the coast in both directions, in sea bathing several times a week and in visiting the Assembly Room where he chose to converse with ladies rather than play at cards.

Skinner left Sidmouth to stay with his friend and fellow clergyman Dr.Flammank, the owner of a small estate near Bodmin. The Flammanks were originally Flemish weavers who settled in Bodmin at the time of Henry II; the last Bodmin Flammanks departed the scene in the last century although their name lives on in Flammank Park, a modern housing estate.

On November 10th, John Skinner and Mr J.Flammank set out on a tour to Land's End. Skinner took a great interest in the mining country about Camborne and

Redruth and in all the particular attributes of a county that is in England but hardly of England. A week later he was in Bodmin once again and a week later still, at home in Claverton. He served here as curate until the autumn of 1799, when he took up a curacy at South Brent, some distance away but in the same county of Somerset.

The following year his uncle, Rector of a parish in Hertfordshire, purchased for him the living of Camerton, a village some six miles south west of Bath on the edge of the Somerset coalfield. This was a boom time for local pits: the population of the parish trebled during Skinner's time there and the colliers and their families were not without their share of problems: namely disease and drunkenness. Skinner had also to contend with a stormy relationship with the local squire. He fulfilled his priestly role with a sense of Christian duty if not unbounded love. As relaxation from parochial preoccupations, he developed his interest in antiquities so that, over the years, there was hardly a site within a wide radius of his parish that had not been investigated by this indefatigable amateur archaeologist. He paid frequent visits to Sir Richard Colt Hoare at Stourhead and kept up a voluminous correspondence, much of it concerned with Skinner's notion that his own parish of Camerton was the site of Camulodunum, one of the first sites of Roman Britain, although all the evidence placed it at Colchester: in this he was opposed by Colt Hoare.

In 1805 he married his beloved Anna and five children were born in the next six years. In 1810 his brother died of consumption and soon after two sisters. In 1811 his three month old daughter, the last child, died of the disease. The following year his wife, too, died of the same cause. The loss of his wife was a tremendous blow. Skinner comes across in his journals as a sensitive and caring man but perhaps without the inner strength and deep faith necessary to sustain one in such a position of responsibility.

While he could make sense of life with the sympathy and understanding of a loving wife, without her he found it increasingly difficult to face up to all the pressures around him, in addition to being left alone with his young family.

Poor Skinner became more and more nervous and bad tempered. His only escape was his archaeology: he wrote copiously of his observations and crackpot theories. In 1820, eight years after the death of his wife, came a further blow: the death from the family disease of his favourite daughter, Laura, a child after his own heart. He certainly loved his remaining children, but found a growing difficulty in living with them. By now his main concern ceased to be the dead past in which he had tended to live, but more himself, and his feelings of persecution.

Portrait of John Skinner, c.1833, by his son Joseph

John Skinner served his parish for another twenty years until, in 1839, his son Joseph taken ill with consumption and John feeling unable to comfort him in his hour of need, he walked out into the wood behind his rectory and shot himself.

Skinner left some 146 volumes of his journals, written between 1788 and 1832, together with 13,000 drawings, to the British Museum. However, some twenty five of the former turned up at a London bookseller's in 1933. Prior to this, in 1930, a selection from Skinner's journals were published by John Murray, under the title, *Journal of a Somerset Rector,* covering the years 1822-32. Kingsmead Press of Bath published an expanded edition covering the years 1803-34 in 1971 and this was reissued as an Oxford University paperback in 1984.

Virginia Woolf wrote an appreciative and sympathetic study of Skinner in her *Common Reader* under the title *Two Parsons* (the other being the contrasting Parson Woodforde). It is a pleasure here to have the opportunity of publishing a hitherto unpublished piece by John Skinner, and one that entertains as well as informs: it comes from the pen of a young man at the threshold of his career and not bowed down by it, with his full health, both of mind and body, and with a curiosity to see, to know, to understand and to record.

Roger Jones
Bradford on Avon
August 1985

Diary of an Excursion through part of Somerset, Devonshire and Cornwall, in the Autumn of 1797

September 20, 1797

Claverton

I left my Mother's house at Claverton, this evening, accompanied by Le Marquis de Kermel, a French Emigrant, designing to reach Wells to sleep, but we were detained the night at Old Down Inn, six miles short of our intended stage, by the rain. As I had often travelled over the same ground, I was the less disappointed, but much regretted my companion could not see the views to advantage. The first part of the way from Bath, is very hilly, on a clear day, commanding extensive prospects on each side of the road; some gentlemen's seats beautifully situated in the vallies diversify the scene. The plantations of Combe Hay, the property of Colonel Smith, are seen to advantage from Dunkerton, near the four mile stone; a little beyond are Camerton and Woodborough, the seats of Messrs Stephens and Purnell. A communication has lately

Somerset Coal Canal

been made in the neighbourhood with the Kennet and Avon Canal, in order to convey Coal to Bath, and different parts of Wiltshire, an undertaking which promises considerable benefit to the Country gentlemen, as some of their estates, supply that commodity in abundance. Descending a steep hill into Radstock valley, and passing through part of the village, we gained the higher ground beyond: the road from

Wells and Glastonbury Tor
View south west from the Mendip Hills

Chilcompton

hence continued tolerable level till we entered Chilcompton, a village prettily situated between the hills. Leaving an old mansion belonging to Major Tucker to the right, we arrived at Old Down Inn, The termination of our Stage for the night.

September 21

Early this morning we crossed the Mendip Hills, breakfasted with my brother William at Wells, I was afterwards examined for Priest's Orders by the Subdean, Mr Moss, who desired me to preach the Ordination Sermon the following Sunday. Wells is pleasantly situated in a fertile Country, at the foot of the Mendip Hills, and I find it was a Bishop's See, as far back as the year 605, and subsequently united to Bath about the year 1138. The Cathedral was originally founded by the Saxon King Ina about the year 704, but such considerable alterations were afterwards made by the then Bishop Fitz Joceline, in the reign of Henry the Second, that it may be almost called his work. It is certainly a beautiful remain of ancient sculpture, and most interesting to the Antiquary, as the West front is decorated with a profusion of images of Kings and Warriors, in the costume of the times. The Chapter House is an elegant structure, having its ornamented roof supported by a single pillar. As the Cathedral stands in an open close, like that at Salisbury, it is seen to more advantage than many on that account. The Deanery and other good houses surround the area, and the Bishop's Palace, situated a little more to the southward, retains its original castellated form, being encompassed by high walls and a moat. The interior is fitted up in a modern style, and appears to be a very comfortable residence, suitable to the revenue of the

Wells Cathedral

Bishop's Palace

See, which at present is computed at nearly six thousand pounds per annum.

Having perambulated this quiet City with my companion till dinner time, we walked in the Evening to a remarkable cavern called Wokey Hole, on the south side of the Mendip Hills, about two miles from Wells, and entered the gloomy region under the direction of a guide who supplied us with candles, and passing a few yards along a passage fifteen or sixteen feet high, found ourselves in a very lofty apartment, whose unequal roof was ornamented by a variety of pointed rocks and petrefactions. Some of these cones, we learnt, were cut off and presented to Mr Pope*, whilst he was engaged in forming his grotto at Twickenham. Gradually descending from the first cavern by a narrow and uneven passage, we entered into another room, not altogether so high, but nearly as long and as wide as the former. From hence continuing our progress over damp and slippery rocks, we came to a third vault, still more contracted in our dimensions. This was the termination of our underground excursion, as a clear stream of water forbid further progress. This water is supposed, I know not on what authority, to flow from Cheddar, eight miles distant, through the centre of the Mendip Hills. It was extremely dark by the time we returned to the Inn.

September 22,23,24

My time was employed in composing and preaching the Ordination Sermon.

---

* The poet Alexander Pope

September 25

Glastonbury

Having taken leave of my companion, who to Bath, I left Wells at twelve, and about five miles beyond, put up my horse, in order to visit the interesting remains at Glastonbury. This celebrated Monastery, majestic even in its decay, is said to have been the first founded, and the last destroyed in the kingdom. According to the Monkish accounts, Joseph of Aramathea, first preached the Gospel here, thirty years after the death of our Saviour, and obtained from King Avaragus twelve hides of land, as a perpetual endowment for twelve devout Christians who for many years after resided on the spot in a hut made with earth and covered with boughs. Be this as it may, we have authentic records, that in the beginning of the fifth Century, a large Society of Monks was established here, and that Arthur, and many of the Saxon Kings were buried within its consecrated ground. It flourished in great splendour till the reign of Henry the Eighth, when Richard Whiting, conscientiously refusing to deliver up the keys to the tyrant, was, through his instigation, accused of High Treason, condemned, and executed. The revenues were then valued at £3311 per Annum, by Dugdale, and at £3580, by Speed.

Glastonbury Tor

On the Torr, a pyramidical hill, near the Monastery, the tower of a Church built by the Abbots, is still preserved as an excellent sea mark, for ships navigating the Bristol Channel: hence the rich domains of the Abbey might be seen extending for miles over the flat country, and here it was that the unfortunate Whiting was hung. I took two hasty sketches, one of the ruins of the Monastery; the second of the Abbot's Kitchen, which continues entire, the roof being constructed entirely of stone, without beams or rafters, because, as my conductor assured me, the King once sent a message to the Abbot, purporting, that if he did not comply with his demands, he would come and burn his Kitchen about his ears; the other replied, he would put that out of his power, and accordingly planned the present structure.

Leaving these interesting remains with reluctance, I proceeded to Bridgewater to dine; this is a large and populous town, situated on the river Parret, which connects it with the Severn. Its trade is considerable, if we may judge from the sloops and barges seen now lying along the quay below the Bridge. The bridge itself is worthy of notice, being one arch of cast iron, nearly an hundred feet in span: it was formed by the Colebrook Dale Company in the year 1792, as we are informed by the date on the railing. Besides its external commerce, considerable manufactories are carried on in the place, amongst which, is a very extensive concern, wherein two or three hundred hands are employed in making Urns, Tea Waiters, and other Japaned articles; the paintings and ornaments here exhibited are in every respect equal to the Birmingham ware of the same kind.

Leaving Bridgewater about six, I arrived at Taunton, twelve miles distant, to sleep. The Country from Wells to Taunton, is very rich, and the roads good.

September 26

Taunton

I walked before breakfast about Taunton, which is cleanly and well built, and noticed in a more particular manner its Church tower of elegant Gothic workmanship. The town is pleasantly situated on the river Thone. It is a populous Borough, thought to be one of the largest in the Kingdom. Ina King of the West Saxons built a Castle here, which was demolished by his wife; but afterwards was rebuilt by one of the Bishops of Winchester, to the Prelates of which See, this Town and Deanery belonged, even before the Conquest. This Castle was a building of great extent, its hall, with the outer gate and Porter's lodge, are still standing, and in the hall, which is very large, the Assizes for the County are generally held. At the entrance into the Court, is the Exchequer, where the Bishop's Clerk keeps his Court, which is held every Saturday for the Bishop's tenants. This Castle was garrisoned by the Parliament in the Civil War, when it was beseiged by Goring; Lord Fairfax marched to relieve it, on which Goring raised the seige, and a few days afterwards was defeated by Fairfax at Langport, who killed several of his men, and took twelve hundred horses, and four-teen hundred prisoners. This victory was followed by the taking Brdigewater, Bath, Sherborne, and Bristol. King Charles the Second in the year 1622*, called its walls to be demolished, and took away the Charter from the town, on account of the inhabitants having adhered to Parliament in the reign of his Father, and they were sixteen years without one, till the same Prince granted them a new one.

There is no prison here, except a Bridewell for vagrants; debtors and criminals being sent to the County Goal at Ilchester. Indeed though this is one of the most flourishing towns in the County, it is the meanest Corporation, for they have neither lands, houses, or joint stock of money.

The Members to serve in Parliament are elected by Pot Wallopers, that is, all who can boil a pot. In consequence of this privilege, the inmates or lodgers, a little before the time of election, have each a fire in the street, at which they publicly dress their victuals, lest their votes should be called in question. The number of

* Should read 1682

inhabitants are computed at twenty thousand, and eleven hundred looms have been employed at a time, in weaving serges, duroys, sagatees, shalloons, and children of five years of age, gain great part of their livelihood in these manufactories.

It ought not to be omitted, that this town suffered greatly by the cruelty of Major General Kirk, immediately after the Duke of Monmouth's defeat in 1685; who being sent hither, caused nineteen persons, by his own authority, without any trial or process, or without suffering their wives or children to speak to them, to be hanged, with pipes playing, drums beating, trumpets sounding. The same inhuman monster, having invited his officers to dinner, ordered thirty persons, condemned here by Jefferies, to be hanged, while they were at table; namely, ten in a health to the King; ten whilst the Queen's health went round; and ten whilst the health passed to Jefferies.

In this town was born Henry Grove*, an elegant writer in the beginning of the eighteenth Century, on the 24th of January, 1683, and educated at the dissenting academy of this place; he removed to London, where he continued about two years, and then returned to the Country, where he commenced preacher at the age of twenty two. About a twelve month after he became a Tutor at the academy where he had been educated, and this with the Dissenting Meeting at Fulwood near Taunton, was the only preferment he ever obtained. He might have risen to much higher dignities, could he have been persuaded to conform to the established Church; but, as this was inconsistent with his principles, he could never be prevailed on to comply with that condition. His abilities however, were really great, and the sweetness of his

* Henry Grove was Minister of Fullwood (or Pitminster), near Taunton and wrote a number of theological works such as The Immateriality of the Soul.

temper, which was irresistably engaging, procured him the friendship of some of the first persons of the age.

Tiverton

Leaving Taunton at ten o'clock, I arrived at Tiverton, twenty miles distant, to dinner and sleep, having been prevented by the rain, from proceeding as I had intended, to Exeter. Tiverton is a very neat town, and inferior only to Taunton in size: it is situated in a pleasant valley, watered by a beautiful stream. The townspeople enjoy the advantage of a good Freeschool, with scholarships and exhibitions to both Universities.

September 27

Exeter

I left Tiverton this morning at seven, and arrived at Exeter to breakfast, having taken in my way a sketch of Bickley Bridge, which with the adjacent Country formed a pleasing landscape. Exeter was originally one of the chief Roman stations in Britain; and great numbers of their Coins and inscriptions have been dug up within the walls; also some tassellated pavements have been discovered, which mark the importance of the place in past ages. At the time of the Norman Conquest, it was still conspicuous and well fortified: part of its old Castle walls still remain, which are rendered interesting from the recollection of past occurences, particularly the gallant seige they sustained in the reign of Henry the Seventh from the rebels, headed by the impostor Perkin Warbeck. The public walks without the City command beautiful and extensive prospects. The healthiness of the Country, connected with the advantages resulting from Commerce, render it in every respect, a most desirable residence for families whose income is small: the only disadvantage which strikes the stranger is, the unevenness of the pavements, in most parts formed of round pebbles, which must render the passing to and fro inconvenient, and in some respects, dirty.

Exeter from Pensylvania Hill

Exeter Cathedral

Within the walls of the City are sixteen Churches, besides Chapels, and five large Meeting Houses, four also are without the walls. The Cathedral, which is dedicated to St Peter, is a stately pile, and though said to have been altogether four hundred years in building, appears as uniform as if it had been erected by one architect. It measures three hundred and ninety feet in length, and seventy four in breadth, having a ring of bells, reckoned the largest in England; as also its Organ, the greatest pipe of which is fifteen inches in diameter. The Dean and Chapter are accomodated with good habitations in the Close near the Cathedral.

Sidmouth

From Exeter I proceeded to Sidmouth, the place of my destination, fifteen miles distant, to dinner: the roads rough, but the views interesting. The place from its low situation on the beach is sheltered and warm, it being surrounded on every side except towards the sea, by high hills ;the pleasantness of its situation of late years, has attracted many bathers, though its beach is by no means so well adapted to the purpose, as a more shelving sandy shore, it being a bank of shingles, or large pebbles, and the sea deep, and at times very rough near the coast. At present, there are but four machines employed, and the gentlemen and ladies, engage them indiscriminately. To remedy in some measure the inconvenience, of the loose beach, the inhabitants , have formed a gravel walk nearly a quarter of a mile in length, facing the sea, which is the usual resort for the company, also a thatched building to shelter them in bad weather, and a billiard table. They have besides, a spacious assembly and card room, where they meet six evenings in the week, during the season, which are in general well attended, the subscription being half a guinea, and two shillings on coming into the room on a ball night. The accomodations at the London Inn are good, and the people civil.

Sidmouth
View from the beach looking west

September 28

Quitting the Inn, I took lodgings at eighteen shillings a week from this day, and agreed for my horse at twelve shillings. During my morning's walk, I happened to meet Mr Amyatt of Southampton, who is staying here with his wife and daughter, and on his telling me it was his intention to visit Exmouth and Teignmouth the following day, I accepted his invitation of accompanying him on his excursion, being anxious to see these bathing places in order to form a proper judgement of the comparative advantages of each.

September 29

Mr Amyatt and myself left Sidmouth this morning at seven o'clock in his carriage; passing a mountain almost perpendicular, called Peak Hill, and traversing a good deal of uneven ground, we arrived at Exmouth about two, and whilst the horses were preparing to cross the ferry, I walked with him to call on a gentleman of the name of Evans, where we found an old acquaintance, Sir John D'Oyly, who had just returned from taking leave of his Son, detained for nearly two months on his passage to India, by contrary winds in Torbay. We were very hospitably entertained, and it was lucky for us, that we laid in some stock of provender, as we did not arrive at Teignmouth till after eight o'clock.

Exmouth

Exmouth, in point of situation and extent is superior to Sidmouth, and the beach appears better adapted for bathing, it being more level. The river Ex, when the tide is in, affords beautiful scenery, Lord Courtney's, Mr Baring's, and many other gentlemen's seats being on the banks, but at low water the smell of the mud must be very unpleasant. I understand the company who frequent this place live more to themselves, than they do at Sidmouth, and in many respects I should think it was a preferable bathing place; however, we found the ferry difficult, and indeed dangerous for carriages; as we crossed in the large boat, the wheels, and part of the perch, hung over the water, and should any sudden blast have taken our broadside in that situation, we should have been in the greatest danger of oversetting. I think they charged Mr Amyatt seven shillings and sixpence for taking over his carriage, besides the fare for the horses.

September 30

Teignmouth

I rose early to perambulate Teignmouth, and bathed; the Country round is very beautiful: there is a public walk on the shore, some hundred yards in length, which commands a view of the sea - it was formed, as at Sidmouth, for the convenience of the company. The assembly room is well fitted up; but not so good in respect of proportion, as that at Sidmouth, it being too long and narrow for its height. This year it has not been so well attended as formerly.

About ten, I crossed in the ferry boat with Mr Amyatt, to a small village called Sharlden, and breakfasted with his nephew, who is there for the benefit of his children's bathing. After breakfast we saw thirteen Salmon caught at one draught. It is peculiar to this place, I believe, that the women alone are employed in the Salmon fishery, there being eight nets in the village, and eight women to each net. Every fourth fish that is caught, is the right of the Lord of the Manor, and every person who chuses to fish, complying with this custom, has permissiom to make use of as many nets as he thinks fit, which the rather surprised me, when I saw none but females; but the men I believe, are chiefly employed in piloting ships, or in other fisheries. These women are dressed in large trowsers, like the Dutch,

Teignmouth
View from Shaldon looking north; ferry in left foreground

and when they are drawing the Seine, they pull off their shoes and stockings, and altogether, are no very captivating syrens. They told me an anecdote of one rather a fine girl, who was put out to service, in a very good place, but never was happy till she returned to her old associates, and she is now engaged with the rest in this laborious manner of gaining her livelihood. About one, we took a boat up the river, having previously called on a Captain Lee, who made us promise to dine with him at half past four.

Teign Estuary

The River Teign affords on both sides of the water very beautiful views, two or three of the most striking, I sketched as we passed along. After rowing about four miles up, we landed at a farm house called Bucklands, formerly the property of Judge Gould's* family, but now of the Countess of Cavan, his daughter. The house at present is not too good for the man who farms the land, but appears to have been larger. From a rising ground near this place is a very beautiful prospect, commanding the river and opposite hills, of which, at Mr Amyatt's request, I took a sketch, which I afterwards finished for him, as he meant to give it to Lady Cavan, who had never seen the place.

It was here I tasted a Devonshire dish, called Squab Pie, the farmer's family being just sat down to dinner on an enormous one, I dare say, four feet in circumference; it is composed of apples, onions, and a neck of mutton, and notwithstanding the mixture may appear singular, it is by no means a bad thing. We arrived at home just time enough to dine with Captain Lee, who is the Father of the handsome Mrs Tickle, and were entertained with great hospitality. The night turning out stormy, we were under the necessity of sleeping at Sharlden, and the next morning, after breakfast, returned to Teignmouth.

---

* Probably Judge Gould, 1726-1806, who became a judge advocate general.

Teign Estuary
View from the south bank looking north toward the Haldon
Hills

October 1

Sidmouth again

We got into the carriage at ten, and returned by the Countess of Ware's bridge, wishing to avoid the ferry at Exmouth. The road seemed beautiful, running by Lord Courtney's and Lord Lisburne's grounds, but could not see their seats to advantage, the weather being foggy. We got home to dine at Sidmouth. I continued at Sidmouth till the first of November, usually bathing four or five times a week, and during this period, taking many pleasant rides around the neighbouring villages. The country is hilly, and in some parts well wooded: the roads, or rather lanes, are deep, and the banks so high, that in passing through them, you see very little of the surrounding scenery; but this is in some respects a beauty rather than an imperfection, as the views, where there are openings, appear to double advantage, the banks of the road forming so fine a foreground, they being generally covered with foliage, which opposed to the red earth, produces a fine contrast in colouring. I think indeed, a painter has more subjects here, and a greater variety of foreground, than in any country I ever saw. The rocks along the coast are of this red cast, as I have endeavoured to shew in my drawings of Sidmouth, and the adjacent shore. With regard to the amusements, as I before observed, there is card playing every night in the week, and dancing on Wednesdays, when they usually collect fourteen or fifteen couple. As I did not play at cards, I often preferred staying at home to going out in the evening; however, when I was in the rooms, I always found some ladies sitting out to converse with.

Provisions, excepting fish, are much the same as in other places; that article is remarkably cheap, as they are brought here in the season, from the neighbouring villages, so that the markets are well stocked. They caught, whilst I was at Sidmouth, upon the beach, at one haul, fifteen hundred large mackarel, some were sold at a penny a piece, in the town, the rest sent to Exeter.

Budleigh Salterton and Dawlish

Between Sidmouth and Exmouth, are two small places on the Coast, to which those who are fonder of retirement resort: Budleigh Salterton and Dawlish; the former is a very small place, and there is, I believe only one bathing machine, and the beach is much like that at Sidmouth: but at Dawlish, they have a smoother shore, and can walk nearly half a mile on the sand; indeed this place has of late become a good deal into fashion, and in a few years perhaps, it may be more frequented than Sidmouth.

Beer and Seaton

Plymouth

On the Dorsetshire side of Sidmouth, are Beere and Seaton, both fishing places, and both inhabited by fishermen; but occasionally resorted to as retired places for bathing, for those who think Lyme and Sidmouth too public. I also made an excursion to Plymouth, taking sketches of Ivybridge and two views of Mount Edgcombe, which are most interesting situations; the one a beautiful rural retirement; the other, a grand prospect, uniting activity of Commerce and Navigation, with most impressive scenery.

WCT–C

November 1

Oakampton

Having received an invitation from my old friend Dr Flammank to spend some days with him in Cornwall, I left Sidmouth at ten o'clock, not stopping till I reached Cockern Well*, twelve miles on the other side of Exeter, in all a twenty seven mile stage; the Country round Exeter is rich and woody, but as you proceed forward, the hills gradually become more barren. I arrived at Oakhampton, eleven miles beyond, to sleep. Its name is derived from the river Oke or Oche, on which it is situated. The town has not much beauty to recommend it; the Innkeeper however, was not deficient in his trade, since I paid more here, and was worse served, than at any other place on the road.

The waiter told me a horrid story of a murder committed in the neighbourhood a few years since; his account was as follows: "A man riding one morning by a small cottage, in which lived three women, grandmother, mother, and daughter, who gained their living by spinning; saw blood running under the door; at which, being much alarmed, he procured assistance, and forced the door; when a scene presented itself, almost too horrid to be mentioned: they were all three found lying dead, in different parts of the room, cut and mangled in a most dreadful manner. For some days, they could form no suspicion of the author of this bloody transaction; till at length, it fell on a man who had been acquainted with the deceased, and assisted them in preparing their wool. He being seen idle about Oakhampton, with a large cut on his hand, was taken before a neighbouring Justice, who, at first said, there was nothing that could attach to this man, as any innocent person, might be in the same predicament,

---

* Crockernwell

*Okehampton Castle
with Dartmoor behind*

and was going to dismiss him, but in the course of further examination, it came out, that he had told one of his neighbours of the murder early in the morning, before the door was broken open. This immediately led to a discovery; since it ws evident, he must have gone out of the window, the door being fastened on the inside. On the Justice's accusing him with it, he confessed it directly, and said, he had committed the murder, in hopes of finding money, as the women had been lately paid for their work; that he had received the cut in struggling with the grand daughter, who at one time had nearly overpowered him. The wretch was condemned, and executed, the following Assizes."

The roads from Cockern Well are very rough the whole stage, owing to the ignorance or inattention of the people employed in making them, since they put for foundation, a large layer of stones, which as the surface wears, project, leaving deep hollows between: this is the more inexcusable in the surveyors of the Turnpikes, as they have the finest materials at hand, and with a little trouble, might have as good roads as any in the kingdom.

November 2

I quitted Oakhampton at eight this morning, the road being still rough and dirty, and arrived at Launceston at twelve, twenty miles distant. Whilst my horse was eating his corn, I took a stroll round the town, and was much interested by what I observed. It is a clean and populous place, pleasantly situated on an eminence; its ruined Castle, naturally attracts the traveller's notice, as well as that of the Antiquary; as it is supposed to be one of the most ancient buildings of the kind in the kingdom. The outer walls are still to be traced to a considerable extent, having the principal entrance to the North East, through a fortified passage upwards of an hundred feet in length. At the end of

Launceston

Launceston

this stood a great gate, the arch of which was pointed, but is now somewhat imperfect. This led to a smaller gate woth a round arch, opening, into the base court, which is partly covered with modern buildings. In the area of the base court, is a lofty hill, of a conical form, which appears to be partly artificial, and partly natural. On the summit of this hill stands the ruins of the Keep or Citadel.

The building of the Castle, has been attributed to William Earl of Morton* and Cornwall, the Son and heir of Robert Earl of Morton, to whom two hundred and eighty eight Manors in this County were given by William the Conqueror. But this opinion is most probably erronious**, as the stile of workmanship exhibited in several parts of the remains, is apparently of a much earlier date. The walls of the Keep, in particular, have every appearance of being more ancient; and from a retrospective view of the events that have happened in this County, the conjecture appears to be fully warranted, that its foundation is as remote as the time of the Britons, who would undoubtedly endeavour to defend their territory both from Roman and Saxon usurpation, by fortifying the most advanced and important situations. The most therefore, that can with certainty be attributed to the above Earl, is, the repairing and extending the fortifications.

Carew, in his Survey of Cornwall, published in 1602, mentions the finding, about sixty years before "of certain leather Coins, in the Castle walls, whose fair stamp, and strong substance, till then resisted the assaults of time". These singular Coins, if they had either been preserved, or their impressions copied, might have thrown some light upon the age of the

* ie. Mortain
** In fact only very little of Mortain's castle survives, most of it being rebuilt at a later date, though the site had been used as a defensive position by both the Britons and the Saxons.

building, as money, of similar substance, was employed by Edward the First, in erecting Carnarvon Castle in Wales, "to spare better bullion". Some Roman Coins, have, according to Borlase, been found in the neighbourhood; so that is is not unlikely that the Romans long had possession of this fortress, as they seldom neglected a post, from which nature and situation might be defended to advantage.

Leaving Launceston at two, and crossing the most dreary moor I ever beheld, where not a tree is to be seen, nor indeed a single habitation, I arrived at Bodmin, a twenty one mile stage, at a little after six: having taken some refreshment, I paid my respects to Dr Flammank about eight o'clock, and feeling myself fatigued, I went early to bed.

Bodmin

November 3

Bodmin

Bodmin is a large place, occupying the northern side of a hill, and consisting principally of one long street, running East and West, some part of which is unevenly paved, the eastern end of it dangerously narrow. Indeed the spirit of improvement has not yet condescended to visit this ancient town; and it appears, that the site of it has been injudiciously changed from the southern to the northern aspect of a hill, and thus exposed to the cutting winds.

In former times, however, it appears to have been of much consequence, being the principal seat of Religion in the western district, and contained a Priory, a Cathedral, and, according to Hals, thirteen Churches, or free Chapels, of which the foundations, and sites of the following still remain, or remembered by some of the inhabitants. The priory, with its Chapel: St Peter's Church: St Paul's, on the north side of the town, a solitary square tower of which still remains: St Nicholas, or the Friary, of which the Town Hall, and Sessions House occupy the Refectory part: St Anthony's Chapel, near Chapel lane: and St Leonard' Church, near the western Turnpike. The first of these religious establishments, was removed from Padstow, where it had been too much exposed to the piracies of the Saxons and Danes.

"The Church", says Whitaker, "is the largest, tallest, and fairest, of all the Cornish Churches". This is very just with respect to the interior, but its extended appearance, will not justify the description, as it is irregular, badly built, and devoid of any architectural beauty. A little to the West of the Church is part of an old building now converted into a school room. This appears to have belonged to the Priory, which was still further to the East; and whose site is occupied by a neat,

Lanhydrock
a National Trust property since 1953

comfortable, modern building, the seat of W. Raleigh Gilbert, Esq., who carefully preserves every relict of antiquity within his power.

Boscarne

This morning I walked with the Dr to his Estate at Boscarne, two miles from Bodmin. The old mansion is prettily situated in a valley, having the river Camel running through the grounds, where they spear a number of Salmon annually: the method of taking them is this: the fishermen watch them in the deep holes under the banks, where they lie quiet in the day time, and dart at them with a barbed spear, attached to the hand by a cord. The fish, if a large one, sometimes swims a great way with the heavy spear in its side, but seldom escapes, except the barb breaks. They also take them by night, by the same means, only burning a little straw on the banks, which entice the fish to the place, and they then watch the opportunity of darting at them.

November 4

Lanhydrock

This morning I took a ride in company with Mr J Flammank, brother to the Dr to Llanhydrock, about three miles East of Bodmin, the seat of Mr Hunt, formerly belonging to the Earls of Radnor. It is a low, though extensive building, anciently a quadrangle, but one of its sides has for some years been taken down. I observed little worthy of notice, excepting two or three paintings Mr Hunt brought from Italy: one of them, a showpiece, appeared to be a masterly composition. From Llanhydrock, we proceeded to view the remains

Restormel Castle

of Restormel Castle, which stands on the summit of a high hill, about a mile North of Lostwithiel. The declivity on the North side is remarkably steep, having its base swept by the rapid water of the Fawy river. This side, and indeed the greatest part of the hill, is covered

Restormel Castle

with a thick mass of wood of diversified character, and variegated foliage.

The rampart, or outer wall of the Castle, is nearly a circle, surrounded with a wide and deep ditch, having a raised terrace on the outside, which commands many views singularly beautiful, from the combination of wood, water, lawn, and meadow; the contour of the hills, and the variety of the receding distances. The entrance to the Castle, is beneath the ruins of a square tower, and an arch more inward. It leads into an open area,between which, and the embattled walls of the ramparts, are a number of different apartments, extending round the whole inside. These were divided into lesser chambers, disposed into two stories, and originally covered with a circular roof, which, however, did not extend over the inner area, the diameter of which, from East to West is sixty eight feet, and from North to South, sixty five.

Lostwithiel

Lostwithiel is a small well built town, and there is a grammar school under the patronage of Lord Mount Edgcombe the present Master, Mr Seley, of Trinity College, Oxford, having gained the appointment through Dr Flammank's interest.

November 5

I rode with the Dr to his Church at Llanhydrock, and officiated for him. The Church is very damp, owing to the windows being made without openings, so that they can let in no air. In the Evening, I read prayers, and preached a Sermon on Idleness, to the prisoners in Bodmin Gaol. This is a large stone building, situated in the side of a hill, and is kept clean and airy. A high wall surrounded it, though not sufficient to prevent the prisoners from escaping, as a short time since, four of them, got away, by the ingenious contrivance of cutting

Bodmin Gaol

their blankets into slips, at the end of which, they fastened an old pocket full of mud, which catching at the top of the wall, enabled them to rise themselves up, and dropping down on the other side, got clear off; but were a few days after again apprehended, and brought back to their old quarters. To remedy the like evils in future, they have removed the cornice of the wall, and rounded it. so that nothing can fasten there, should others be tempted to try the same experiment.

There are some good regulations in the prison, the chief of which is, that none are suffered to remain idle, the women being employed in spinning and weaving, a small profit being allowed them out of their labour; and the men, either in working in the garden, or in polishing the moorstone for chimney pieces. But there is one objection I think, to be made to this, though I know not how it can easily be remedied, and this is, they are all together, I mean the debtors and the others, who are put in for more weighty faults. I saw a woman, not twenty years old, who had been tried three times; and is at present confined for stealing goods out of a house; spinning with a number of other women, whose offences were comparatively very small, such as selling smuggled Gin, etc. In such instances, Howard's plan might be adopted with some effect; it might be more troublesome, but it would certainly prevent evil communication, and stamp a difference between offences, of which the common people seem to have but little idea. There was a woman to be tried for horse stealing, rather an extraordinary crime for a female.

November 6

This morning was occupied in a ride to Wade Bridge, seven miles West of Bodmin. In my way thither I passed through the village of Egloshaile, the Living of Sir Henry Trelawney, who, usually, I believe, resides at the Parsonage, in preference to Trelawney Castle. This gentleman is by all accounts a singular character, but amongst all his peculiarities, is a good man. He is much followed as a preacher, and, I believe, generally *Wadebridge* delivers his discourses extempore. The Church, as well as the Parsonage, lies low, and at high tides, the water washes the walls. Wadebridge, the largest in the County, has sixteen arches, and is built on a marshy swamp; it was about two Centuries ago undertaken and finished by the Clergymen of the Parish, notwithstanding he met with many difficulties in accomplishing his enterprise, owing to his not being able to find a good foundation, as well as frequently being in want of money to carry it on; however, by perseverence, and the voluntary contributions of some of the neighbouring gentlemen, he was enabled at length to finish it. There is a pretty village near the spot which also bears the name of Wade's bridge. The river Camel gains the sea four miles beyond, is navigable only at high water, and then only for small craft.

November 7

I again accompanied the Dr to Boscarne, and in the Evening dined with his brother in law Mr Philips, who, on a curacy of forty pounds a year, and a very small private fortune, has bought up a family of nine *Bodmin Assembly* children. After dinner, we went to the Assembly at Bodmin, a monthly meeting, collected at the moderate subscription of five shillings each for the season. The entertainment, as may be supposed, does not discredit this vast expense; the dancing room being not thirty feet long, and the boards laid the contrary way, and very uneven, which occasions various trippings in going down the dance. We found the chamber lighted by five or six candles, stuck against the wall; the Orchestra is usually composed of a blind fidler, and a little scraper his son, but this evening we were more honoured, having the Band of the Somerset Militia, who not only occupied half the room, but stunned us with the noise of their drums, clarionets, etc, etc; indeed I should have been much better pleased, if Mr Fidler had reigned alone. The ladies, however seemed perfectly charmed and contented. To be sure everything is by comparison, and those who have never witnessed a better ballroom, have no reason to be dissatisfied. However I was glad to get away soon after the second dance, leaving the damsels to the more agreeable society of the red coats, amongst whom was Smith of Combe Hay, their Colonel.

November 8

St Roche's Rock

My ride for the day was in company with Mr J Flammank to St Roche's rock, seven miles from Bodmin. This singular curiosity consists of an insulated mass of stone, standing on a heathy plain, retaining the remains of an hermitage or Chapel on its summit. The building partly consists of the natural rocks, and is formed of square stone: it contained two rooms one above the other. The side and end walls still remain, but the floor and roof are destroyed. It appears by the fanciful description given by Morden of these rocks, to have been roofed in his time: "In this rugged pile", says the author, "may be observed five severall workes: the firste of nature, whoe, as a mother, begate this stoneye substance; the next of force, whereby the water at the generall flude depryved it of her earth covering shelter, leavinge it naked; the thirde of arte, which raysed a building upon so rugged a foundation; fourth, of industrye, in workinge concavetye in so obdurate a subjecte; lastlye, of devotion, wherein men, in their then well meeninge zeale, woulde abandon as it were, the societye of human creatures, and undergo the tedious daylie ascent and continuance in so colde and abandoned a place. To this may be added a sixth worke, even of time, who, as she is the mother and begetteth, so she is the destroyer of her begotten children, and nothing that she bringeth forth is perma-nent". The walls of the building are plastered on the inside, the lower room measuring about nine feet by twelve. The whole height of the rock and building may be estimated at about one hundred and twenty feet from the level ground. In one of the fragments of the rocks, there is an aperture, perhaps six inches over, which is always full of water, and one of the country people told me, he remembered when a stream ran from it, and on attempting to fathom it with a long stick, they found no bottom; but now it appears almost choaked up with stones, which have been thrown into it: this they call the Hermit's well. We dined with a Mr Edyvane, a gentleman farmer, and were very hospit-ably entertained.

November 9

This being a rainy day, I staid within doors, penning in the sketches I had taken, to prevent their rubbing out.

November 10

St Michell

Zelah

Redruth

At eight o'clock I set out, accompanied by Mr J Flammank, on a Tour to Land's End, he having obligingly offered to accompany me, as I wished not to miss the opportunity of seeing a Country, I never perhaps may visit again. After riding fifteen miles over a barren heath, we baited our horses at St Michell, which is a mean inconsiderable place, consisting of a few cottages, but returns two members to parliament. The borough is now at the disposal I believe of Sir Christopher Hawkins.

Continuing our route, we passed through a place called Zelah, which is not more prepossessing in respect to building and situation, and then came into the Mining Country: all here is barrenness in the extreme. The miners' cottages scattered up and down; the steam engines; and the wheels for drawing up the buckets, being the only objects we saw for miles. The ground is everywhere covered with heath, which they cut for fuel, a sad substitute for more substantial materials. We passed four Barrows on the hills, of small dimensions; indeed, I had before observed several hillocks of this description, some of which, I understood from my companion, have of late years been opened, and were found to contain Roman Coins; fragments of swords, arms, and remains of the dead. We arrived at Redruth, a little after two. This is a tolerably populous town, chiefly consisting of one long paved street situated on the side of an eminence in the very bosom of the mining district. According to Dr Pryce, its antiquity is superior to that of any other town in the County, and, he observes that its name (Dredruith) is so very ancient, as to be given to the situation of this town, before the kingdom was divided into Parishes, as old writings express it thus: "In the Parish of Uny juxta Dre-druith". But however remote the origin of this place, it does not appear to have arisen to any consequence, till the discovery and working of the Copper Mines, which have been the means of augmenting its population in more than sixfold proportion during the course of the last Century. This is apparent from the number of baptisms, which in the year 1700, amounted to only thirty four; but in 1800*, it was increased to one hundred and ninety six, and for several preceding years it has been somewhat higher. The returns for the town and parish, made under the last act, the inhabitants were enumerated at 2287 males, and 2637 females, and the houses at 664.

The Charter for a Market, and two annual Fairs, was granted by Charles the Second to the family of James Bulley, Esq, of Downs in the County of Devon, who now receives the tolls. Here is also a third fair, held annually in a place called Fair Meadow: this was granted in the time of Henry the Seventh, to the Bassetts of Tehidy, and now belongs to Lord De Dunstanville. Many of the mining transactions are carried on in this town, which in reality derives its whole importance from its centrical situation to the Mines. The Church is a neat modern edifice, about a mile from the town, consisting of a nave only, with a flat ceiling supported by pillars. At this place I delivered a letter of introduction to a Quaker of the name of *Carnbre* Jenkins, who, immediately walked with us to Carnbre, about a mile distant, and which I think is one of the greatest curiosities in the County.

It is a high hill, on the summit and sides of which, are immense fragments of rocks, about fifty, or an hundred tons weight, scattered up and down by some great convulsion of nature; some lying single, others piled

* This postdates Skinner's tour; the diary was presumably written, or more likely a fair copy made, with at least three years hindsight.

Carn Brea, near Redruth
Here can be found traces of prehistoric and Roman
occupation, of a medieval cliff-castle and chapel, and an
eighteenth century monument to Lord de Dunstanville

together with all the appearance of art. On the very apex, is a square castellated building, which bears the marks of antiquity, but there is a more modern addition, built within these forty years, as a Lodge for Free Masons. From this spot you enjoy a prospect of the surrounding country, which is in every respect grand and impressive. This commanding situation, connected with the rude remains you everywhere observe, as you explore the objects more immediately at hand, undoubtedly confirms the opinion that the hill was selected by the Druids as sacred to their rites. The whole base of the hill seems to have been surrounded by a stone wall three miles in circumference, still in parts entire, in order to separate the sacred ground from the profane. Procul O procul este profani! An inpenetrable grove of oaks, the remains of which may yet be traced, in all probability more effectually concealed their sanguinary mysteries.

I took two sketches on the spot, and the evening closing in, we separated from our friend the Quaker who, instead of the usual stiffness peculiar to his sect, was possessed of more real politeness, than is in general to be met with in the world; he not only pressed us to spend the evening with him, but declared, had he not a great deal of business on his hands, he would himself have accompanied us to Land's End. In the course of conversation, he informed us, that Dr Jackson*, Dean of Christ Church, Oxford, had visited this place last year, and that he had attended him in his walks, and expressed himself much pleased with the Doctor's company, and with the sagacious observations he made. We mounted our horses about six, and arrived at Cambron, four miles beyond, to a late dinner and to sleep.

Cambron

---

* Cyril Jackson, 1746-1819, had acted as a sub-precentor to the two eldest sons of George III until dismissed; was a botanist and student of architecture.

November 11

Tehidy

We breakfasted with Kegwin, an old College acquaintance, who at present resides on the Curacy of Cambron, and rode in his company to Tehidy the Seat of Lord De Dunstanville and Basset. The mansion is situated about four miles North West of Redruth, and when seen from Carnbre hill, appears like a well cultivated garden, in the midst of a sterile desert. Its spreading woods are beheld with additional delight, from the contrasted scenery of the surrounding Country, where the face of nature has been robbed of all ornament, and the interior of the earth, if I may be permitted the expression, been scattered over its surface, in pursuit of ore.

The Manor house was erected by John Pendarvis Basset, Esq, Uncle to the present proprietor; from designs by Edwards. The buildings are chiefly constructed of Cornish freestone, and consist of a square and spacious dwelling house in the centre, and four detatched pavilions at the angles. The pavilions contain the domestic offices, and a private Chapel. On the summit of the house is a statue of the Farnese Flora executed in Coade's stone.

The whole extent of the park and grounds is about seven hundred acres, of which one hundred and fifty are appropriated to a Lawn and sheep walk, and one hundred and thirty to woodland, ninety of which have been planted by the present Nobleman, by whom the Estate has been greatly improved, and many judicious alterations effected. The number of trees planted annually for the last twenty years, have been varied from five to ten thousand, and from that to between thirty and forty thousand. The pine clusters, are constantly planted as screens for the other trees, which are here not set in the ground till the former have attained two years growth. Silver Firs, Laurels, both common and Portugal, Holly, and Cypresses; answer extremely well. Of deciduous trees, the Oak, Spanish Chestnut, Beech, and Sycamore, flourish best; the Larch will not succeed unless in very sheltered spots.

Hayle

From this place, we proceeded along the cliffs, (one of which called Hayle's mouth I sketched) to Hayle, and passed by a large Copper house belonging to the Copper Company in London. In the way, is a remarkable sand bank, for a mile or two long, thrown up by the sea, though at present at a great distance from high water mark, which proves that the Coast gains on this side. The sand they use for manure, it being composed in a great measure of very fine shells which are of great benefit to a very stiff soil. From Hayle, riding along the

Tredea

beach, we came to Tredea, the residence of Mr Giddy, whom I remember to have seen at Oxford, a Gentleman Commoner of Pembroke College. He was then generally pointed out as a Ralph, as the elegant phraise is, for one who is not attentive to his dress, but this very Ralph may chance to have his name remembered when the fine gentlemen who were so proud of their fancied superiority are no more heard of, as he is generally esteemed a good scholar, and turns his studies chiefly to the mathematics, and possesses the greatest collection of books on that science I ever saw in a private library. To be sure his dress and address are not very prepossessing, but I am sure in real civility he is not at all deficient. I should much have liked to have accepted his invitation to spend the day with him, but being straightened for time, we were obliged to take our

Marazion

leave, and proceed to Marazion or Jew's Market, which is a small town built on the side, and at the bottom of a hill, which rises towards the North, and shelterd it from the cold winds. Peculiarity of situation, and the mildness of the western climate, renders this vicinity singularly inviting, and often beneficial to valetudinarians, and were it not for the frequent rains that occur in this part of the country, the invalid would have little occasion to travel to Italy, or the South of France for a mild and salubrious atmosphere. Its trade consists principally in importing timber, coals, and iron for the use of the neighbouring mines. The Parish Church, that of St Hilary, is about two miles distant; but the town has a Chapel of Ease, in which service is regularly performed by a Lecturer, whose salary is defrayed by private subscription.

Chapel Rock

Between Marazion and St Michael's Mount, is a place called Chapel Rock, whereon the pilgrims who came to visit the Priory of St Michael's are said to have performed certain devotionary and superstitious ceremonies in a kind of initiatory Chapel, previous to their admission to the sacred Mount and situated just opposite to Marazion is the far famed Mount, which is one of those rare and commanding objects that arrest and fix the attention the moment they are seen. Its peculiar situation, and the sublime character it assumes, from appearing to rise immediately from the waves, singularly interest the imagination of the observer, though when viewed from the land, its real magnitude is apparently diminished, from the vast extent of the horizon, and the expanded tract of the water which surrounds its base. At high water, it appears a completely insulated congregation of rocks, towering to a considerable height, gradually decreasing in size, till assisted by the tower of the Chapel on its summit, it assumes the form of a complete pyramid. At low water, it is approached from the shore by a kind of causeway of sand, and rocks, which are submerged by every rising tide, and the Mount rendered again a perfect Island. Some of the masses of rocks in the intermediate space, are immensely large, and all composed of granite of a close texture, which is a felspar of

St Michael's Mount

St Michael's Mount
Largely rebuilt in the 1870s, though much remains of the
medieval period; now belongs to the National Trust

a pinkish colour. The Mount itself, "consists of a hard granite, in which transparent quartz is the predominating substance". From various stations, its appearance is different; being in some places nearly perpendicular; and at others of a gentle declivity; and though the rocks are for the most part craggy and barren, yet the soil affords sufficient herbage to pasture a score of sheep or upwards, for a whole year.

The Mount, in the remote ages of Antiquity, is supposed by some to have been situated in a wood; a circumstance to which its name in the Cornish language gives a considerable degree of probability. Its Cornish appellation was Carak-ludgh en lux, signifying the grey or hoary rock in the wood. The tradition is partly confirmed by the testimony of Leland, who remarks that "in the baye betwyxt the mont, and Pensants, be found neere lowe water marke, rootes of trees yn dyvers places".

It is certain that the Mount became hallowed at a very early period, that it was renowned for its sanctity, and was for a time the object of frequent pilgrimage.

When it was first consecrated for religious purposes, is unknown; but the earliest time it appears upon record as a place of devotion, is the fifth Century, though it seems probable that it was then highly celebrated; as St Keyma*, a holy Virgin, of the British blood Royal, and daughter of Brogenus, Prince of Brecknockshire, is stated to have come here on a pilgrimage, about the year 490. Here she was joined by her nephew Cadoc, who is reputed to have made a fountain spring up in a dry place, on which a Church was erected to his honour. Upwards of five hundred years afterwards, Edward the Confessor founded on this spot, a Priory of Benedictine Monks, on whom he

* ie. St Keyne: "sixth century (?), the legend recorded in the fourteenth century makes her a maiden who was both a recluse and an itinerant evangelist" - (Penguin Dictionary of Saints).

bestowed the property of the Mount, together with several other places.

The civil contentions, in the reign of Charles the First, were the cause of the fortifications on the Mount being increased, till, in a Chronicle of the proceedings of the times "the works were styled impregnable and almost inaccessible". They were, however, reduced, after being vigorously defended by the King's adherents, in the Month of April, 1646, by Colonel Hammond, who obtained much celebrity for having accomplished this service, which the Historians of that period represent as full of difficulty and danger.

Many of the improvements that have been effected on the rock, and the increase of the buildings, is to be attributed to Sir John St Aubyn, grandfather to the present Baronet, who in the years 1726 and 1727, rebuilt and enlarged the Piers on the North side of the Mount, and rendered it sufficiently capacious, to contain upwards of fifty sail of small vessels. The security this gave to the fishing boats, induced several of the inhabitants of Marazion to erect houses and cellars at the bottom of the rock, and the number of residences since, have been augmented to seventy. The inhabitants are about two hundred and fifty, and in the Pilchard season the number is increased to three hundred and fifty.

The ascent to the top of the Mount is by a steep and craggy passage, fronting the North, defended about midway by a small battery, and near the summit by the North flank of the principal battery, which also protects the entrance of the Bay. The whole summit is occupied by the remains of the ancient monastic buildings, which were considerably altered by the late proprietor, and have been much improved and beautified by the present possessor, under whose directions the Chapel is now repairing. This is spacious, and of the Gothic order: a staircase, extremely

St Michael's Chapel

Chevy Chase Room

narrow, leads from one of the angles of the tower to the summit, whence the prospect comprehends the entire view of the Bay, the several towns and villages that skirt the Coast, and an immense extent of Sea. Near the Chapel is a spacious apartment, formerly the refectory to the Monastery; this, now called Chevy Chase room, is ornamented with a singular frieze, representing in stucco, the modes of hunting the wild boar, bull, stag, ostridge, fox, hare, and rabbit. At the upper end of the room is the Royal arms, with the date 1644; and at the opposite end, the arms of the St Aubyn family. The various improvements that have been effected on this spot, and the singularity of situation, have rendered it a very convenient and interesting summer residence, and the present proprietor makes it his occasional abode. Formerly, a scarcity of water was occasionally experienced, as there was no other for use than rain water, collected by drains; but about forty years since, a well was sunk through a very hard rock, and a fine spring found at the depth of thirty seven feet, in the immediate vicinity of a tin lode. Specimens of tin ore are said to be very plentiful all over the Mount, in digging for which, human bones and skulls are frequently found where the soil is of sufficient depth for internment.

Pilchard Fishery

The circumference of St Michael's Mount is rather more than a mile; and its height from the sand to the top of the Chapel tower, is ascertained by Hadley's quadrant, to be two hundred and fifty feet. Its distance from the shore at Marazion is about four hundred yards. Nearly all the inhabitants are employed in the different branches of the pilchard fishery, the various operations of which, as carried on in the Bay, become a very interesting spectacle to the traveller, who is induced to visit this part of the Coast, and are thus described by one of very accurate observation:

The craft requisite for an undertaking in this fishery, are as follows: a stop sein, or net, with lead weights at the bottom, and corks at top; the cost of which is about £350. An open boat for carrying the sein, of about fifteen tons burthen, cost £52.10s. Another open boat of similar tonage, to assist in inclosing the fish, cost £52.10s. A smaller boat, to carry the men to and fro from the shore, to assist in other general purposes, cost £25. One or two boats, for carrying the fish to the shore, cost £70, each. A Tuck Sein, made to the stop sein 108 fathoms long, and 10 deep, cost £20. Many other things are also necessary; and the expences of the first outset may be estimated at one thousand or twelve hundred pounds, exclusive of salt.

The number of men employed on a sein, varies from seventeen to twenty four; the average may be set at nineteen. The modes of compensation are also different in different fishing places; but the general amount is nearly the same. At Newkey they have seven shillings a week, and one fourth of the net proceeds of fish and oil; and the fish being on the spot, the general sum obtained by the fishermen is from fifteen to twenty five pounds each man, exclusive of wages.

The season commences about the middle of July, and continues about ten weeks, when the pilchards disappear. The quantity that may be taken depends upon circumstances; such as, whether the fish come within the depth of the sein, the weather, and the strength of the tides, which frequently break the nets, and set the fish at liberty after they are inclosed. Many accidents, though very large quantities are often lost, occur from various other circumstances.

In some instances a sein will take and cure from one thousand to fifteen hundred hogsheads and upwards in a season, when at the same time, some of the neighbouring seins have not a single fish; though it is not uncommon for the above quantity to be inclosed in a single sein at one time. The whole quantity taken in a season, may be estimated at from forty to sixty thousand hogsheads, of forty gallons each, and three thousand fish in each cask.

The pilchards pass the coast in large shoals; and when within the depth of the sein, the boat containing it is rowed round them, the net being thrown over them at the same time: by this means, the fish are surrounded with the stop sein, both ends of which are then fastened together. The bottom of the net is kept to the ground by the lead weights; but the corks keep the top of it floating on the surface of the water.

At low water, the fish are taken up with the Tuck Sein, and carried to the cellars, or store houses, where they are salted and ranged in heaps from five to six feet high, and in some instances ten or twelve feet wide. When a large quantity of fish are inclosed in the stop sein, it sometimes requires two or three weeks to take them out, as they must not be removed in greater quantities than the women who salt them can conveniently manage. In the course of this time, the occurrences of various accidents occasions many fish to be lost, to the collective amount of several thousand pounds annually.

When the fish are taken out of the salt, and packed in hogsheads, they are pressed very hard, with great weights, by the power of a strong lever. By which means the oil is extracted, which runs out of the casks through holes made for the purpose. The pressing continues about fourteen days, when the hogsheads are headed up, and the fish are fit for the merchants.

Some fish are more considerably productive than others of oil: those taken in the early part of the season, in general produce the most, but the fish taken in the latter part, are commonly the best. Forty eight hogsheads of pilchards generally yield a ton or two hundred and fifty two gallons of oil, the price of which is now from twenty four to twenty five pounds per ton: but previous to the late war, it was considerably cheaper, and will probably again decrease in size.

The quantity of salt necessary to cure a hogshead of fish, is about four hundred and twenty pounds; on this is an import duty of about two pence halfpenny per bushel of eighty four pounds. The expences of curing a hogshead of fish, for a cask, labour, salt, etc, is from twenty one to twenty three shillings. On this, the charge for salt alone is six shillings. The fish have been lately sold from thirty five to forty two shillings per hogshead, inclusive of the bounty of eight shillings on exportation. The bounty has latterly been extended to those intended for home consumption. The usual quantity of the salt provided for each sein is three thousand bushels.

The number of persons employed in salting, packing, pressing, and preparing the fish for exportation, is at least five thousand. About four fifths are women, and the rest men. The ropemakers, blacksmiths, shipwrights, sail makers, etc, are upwards of four hundred. The twine spinners are women, about one hundred and fifty in number. The makers and menders of nets are chiefly women and children, employed by the twine manufacturers, and in all about six hundred. Nets are also made, during the winter season, by the fishermen and their families.

These numbers are exclusive of the seamen employed in the shipping, and exportation of the produce of this fishery, which is almost wholly consigned to Italy. Some attempts have been lately made to open a market for pilchards with the metropolis; but the quantity hitherto sold has been insufficient to defray the expences. The capital engaged in this trade is at least three hundred thousand pounds. reckoning the seins, nets, boats, etc, at a fair appraisement, and making every allowance for wear. The original cost must have been considerably more.

Penzance

From Marazion, we rode over a fine hard sand to Penzance, where we arrived about five o'clock. Penzance, a name signifying the head of the Bay, is the most westerly town in England, being situated on the North West side of Mount's Bay, 283 miles from London, and about ten from Land's End. It is particularly distinguished for its cheap fish Market, and the mildness of its seasons, and the fertility of the neighbouring lands, which in some instances have been let so high as twelve or thirteen pounds an acre; and even the average rental of the land, in the vicinity of the town, may be fairly estimated at seven pounds; this is a convincing proof that the soil is either of a superior native quality, or derives some considerable advantage from situation; and these circumstances connected with other local peculiarities, have occasioned a considerable increase of population, by the influx of the inhabitants, from the neighbouring villages.

In Carew's survey, Penzance is represented as "not regardable for his substance is memorable for his late accident of the Spaniards firing", when a few of them invaded Cornwall in the year 1595, and "were the only Spaniards", says Camden, "that ever set foot in England as enemies". They did not, however, acquire many laurels, though for a few days, their incursions spread considerable alarm, through this part of the Country. Their predatory visit is thus described:

Spain, at this period, being mistress of Britagne, whence four gallies were dispatched to invade the English Coast. On the 26th July, they landed near Mouse hole, and commenced their depredations, by burning several houses, the Church of St Paul, and

Penzance
Looking up Market Jew Street before The Market House and
statue of Sir Humphrey Davy were ereced (1837)

afterwards Mousehole itself. Meeting with little resistance, they proceeded to Newlyn, and afterwards to Penzance, where Sir Francis Godolphin had ordered the inhabitants to assemble in the Market place, but when he himself arrived, he found, says Carew "only two resolute shot, which stood at his command, and some ten or twelve others that followed him, most of them his own servants: the rest surprized with feare, fled, whom neither by his persuasions, nor threatening with his rapier drawn, hee could recall". Thus situated Sir Francis was obliged to desert the town to the enemy, who entered at three different places, and set it on fire: and having also burnt Newlyn, returned to their gallies. The next day, they seemed to meditate a fresh landing; but the numbers of the Cornish being augmented, and their courage increased proportionably, the Spaniards desisted; and finding themselves annoyed by the "bullets and arrowes", from the shore, removed to a greater distance, and on the day following, sought security in flight, as means were preparing to interrupt them. The enterprize of the Spaniards appears from Carew, to have been favoured by a prophecy, believed by the vulgar in the Cornish language, which intimated that those should land upon the rock of Merlin, who should burn St Paul's, Penzance, and Newlyn; "and indeed", continues our author, "so is the rocke called where the enemy first stept on shore".

The town from this time seems to have increased both in size and population; and the inhabitants were induced to erect a Chapel of Ease, nearer home, as the Mother, or Parish Church, is situated at Madern, or Maddron, nearly two miles to the Westward. The Chapel is dedicated to St.Mary, and furnished with a small whitewashed spire. Among the various religious sects residing here, may be specified, Methodists,

Quakers, Presbyterians, and Jews; each having a separate place of worship. The government of Penzance is vested in a Mayor, Recorder, twelve Aldermen, and twenty four Common Council men. The streets are paved: many of the houses are large and respectable habitations: and about forty years ago, a new Pier was erected at the expense of the Corporation, unaided by any Parliamentary grant.

A very considerable export trade in tin and pilchards is carried on from hence, and besides a number of fishing vessels always lying in the commodious Bay; Frigates and Excise Cutters are always stationed here, to watch the Smugglers, who in defence of the laws, and regardless of their agents, prosecute their illicit traffic on the Coast with extraordinary audacity and success; and the various stratagems they employ in landing and securing their liquors, furnish singular instances of sagacity and cunning. The exertions of Magistrates, Excise Officers, and Soldiers are equally inefficient to suppress this clandestine trade; and although severe penalties are inflicted on the detected, in almost every Session, yet their successful proceedings furnishes a constant theme of conversation in most parts of the County.

November 12, Sunday

St. Just

As we had a letter to a man who was to accompany us to Land's End, who lived at St.Just, about ten miles distant, we determined on going there today, under the idea of being sure to find him, it being a leisure day, as in the week days he is employed in overlooking the Mines. We arrived at St.Just, just in time for Church; Mr J. Flammank being acquainted with the Clergyman, read Prayers for him. I was surprised to see so large a congregation, and heard some of the best singing I ever remember in a Country Church. I understand that there are sometimes fifteen hundred people assembled here during divine service, it being in the midst of the Mine Country, and what is more extraordinary, the Miners usually attend Meeting before they come to Church, and afterwards, conclude the day by praying and exhorting each other in their own houses. I was much gratified to find this show of Religion among people, one would expect to be most negligent of it (some of them at least) being so far removed from religious instruction. The Curate who has the charge of this extensive Parish only receives £35 per annum, but has just complained to the Bishop, requesting an increase of salary. Many

Prehistoric Remains

barrows are in neighbourhood, and on opening one not long since, a great number of Urns were discovered; and near the centre, a square chest, or cistfaen paved beneath, in which was found an ornamented Urn full of human bones. It is supposed there were fifty other Urns round the stone chest; the abovementioned being preserved, on account of its elegance; the rest were thrown away, and broken as of no consequence. Most of these Urns stood erect on their bottoms, and were covered with a flat stone or tile; but some appeared themselves to be a covering to what they contained, having their mouths placed downwards. This Barrow was probably a family burying place for some Chieftain residing near the spot. Besides these, near the Church at St.Just, might be traced a circular elevation, supposed to have been a theatre, or Gymnasium of the Britons. It was an exact Circle, one hundred and twenty six feet in diameter, and the perpendicular height of the bank from the area within, seven feet, but the height from the bottom of the ditch without, ten feet, though it was formerly more. The seats consisted of six steps, fourteen inches wide and one foot high; and on the top of all, where the rampart is, is about seven feet wide.

The Plays latterly acted in these amphitheatres were in the Cornish language, and the subjects were taken from Scripture History. In the same cirques were also performed those sorts of exercises for which the Cornish Britons are still so remarkable; and indeed, if any single combat was to be fought on foot, to decide any competition of strength or valour, any disputed property, or accusation exhibited by martial challenge, no place was so proper as one of these inclosed circles; but in case of sudden challenges, where the champions were to fight it out upon the spot, the area was marked out with such stones as were at hand. If either combatant, was by any accident, forced out of the circle, he was to lose his cause, and pay three marks of pure silver to save his life.

Cornish Wrestling

In this parish, were also some very ancient Mines, which is not to be wondered at, if we reflect that this coast is within sight of the Cassiterides, or Scilly Isles, and was probably resorted to as one of them by the ancient traders in tin. Having explored all that was worthy of notice at St.Just, we proceed under the direction of our guide to Land's End, about six miles

Lands End

distant. This is the most westerly promontory in England, and exhibits a mass of rock rising majestically from the waves. The strata of these rocks run so even that you may almost fancy they are indebted to the chissel for their smooth surface, and that they were piled one on the other by the gigantic efforts of human architects. The sea view from this rocky promontory is very grand, and the eye reposes with pleasure on the lighthouse, built on some detached rocks out at Sea, called the Long Ships, to warn off sailors from this dangerous shore.

Logan Stone

Having taken a rough sketch, we remounted our horses, bestowing a trifle on some youngsters who had nearly ran a mile to hold them, and trotted on to the Logan Stone, five miles further along the coast. In our way we had an opportunity of seeing the Scilly Isles; the evening being remarkably clear, our guide, who had formerly been a smuggler, but changed his way of living through scruples of conscience, and in his occupation had frequently visited these Islands, gave so interesting a description of the surprising things to be seen there, that although it was late in the year, we determined to cross over thither; especially as he informed us, there were passage boats passing weekly from Penzance. We arrived at the Logan Stone about four o'clock. This Druidical remain, for, I believe it is pretty fully ascertained that all the Logan or Rocking Stones were constructed to further the superstitious views of this race of men, strikes you at once with awe as you approach it. Although fifty or sixty tons in weight it stands so equally poised, on a summit of a vast pile of rocks that you may move it backward and forward with your hand; and yet, notwithstanding the great facility with which it is moved, it cannot be thrown from its centre, as was proved by the attempts of some Miners a little while ago, who wantonly tried, with the assistance of levers, and their united strength to throw it into the sea; but fortunately were not able to succeed in their purpose. Sometimes from the crumbling away of the stone, and the small pieces falling underneath: the groove in which it rests is choaked up, and the mass for a time immoveable, at least to the hand, but when these particles are ground to dust, by the rocking of the stone in stormy weather, it is then as easy to be moved as before. At the time I saw it, it was not only put in motion by the hand, but might be continued moving by the touch of a single finger, as Mr J.Flammank tried.

The way to climb up to this stone is difficult, and dangerous, for if your foot slips, you must, in all probability, fall into the sea. Having taken a sketch of this stone, as well as of some of the surrounding rocks, called Castle Treryn, and the evening closing in we made the best of our way back to Penzance, our companion, the quondam smuggler returning to St Just; indeed, without his assistance, we should have experienced great difficulty, it being ten miles thither, along a bad road, and the night remarkably dark; as it was, we did not arrive at the Inn till nine o'clock. On inquiring, we found that the passage boat had sailed the day before to the Scilly Isles; and learning also, that if the wind happened to change, we might be detained there a week or fortnight, we determined, though not without reluctance on our part, as well as the smuggler's who had promised to be our guide thither, to put off our intended excursion. Should I ever return to Cornwall, it would be my first object to visit these remarkable, those little explored islands.

November 13

After breakfast, whilst walking on the quay, I entered into conversation with a Dutch Captain; who commands a neutral ship, trading in pilchards, and was pleased to find, I could make myself understood, though I have not spoken the Dutch language these eight years. The quay is very commodious, even for vessels of large burthen, which can load and unload, without any interruption from the winds or tide.

Helston

I left Penzance about twelve, and arrived at Helston a little after two. The road in parts is very picturesque, the cliffs and sea on the right hand, frequently affording fine views. The town is large and populous, situated on the side of a hill, which slopes gradually to the little river Cober. The houses are chiefly disposed in four streets, and near the middle of the principal one, is the Market House, and Town Hall. On an eminence to the North, stands the Church: this was erected about the year 1762, and from its elevated situation, and lofty pinnacled Tower, forms a very fine object, from many parts of the valley lying between it and the sea. Though this is one of the original Stannary towns, very little tin is now coined here. The old Coinage Hall, is inhabited by an Officer of the Duchy to which the Manor originally belonged. The Manor was sold to redeem the Land Tax in the year 1798, and purchased by John Rogers, Esq., the present Recorder of the Borough.

It being a wet evening, we continued at Helston, where we found good accomodations at the Inn, and we left it a little after ten on the 14th in order to visit Looe Pool, which is a beautiful piece of water, belonging to the above mentioned Mr Rogers. This gentleman's house, called Penrose, is situated in the midst of a finely wooded scene about two miles from the Town, on the borders of the Lake which is everywhere a fine

Penrose

Penrose, and Loe Pool, near Helston
The largest lake in Cornwall whose waters are now controlled
by a sluice gate at the seaward end

Looe Pool

object from his grounds. The waves of the British Channel operating strongly on this part of the Coast, forces a great quantity of sand and pebbles, which are constantly accumulating, forms a thick and high bank or dam, extending across the valley from hill to hill, and by closing the mouth of the river, occasions it to spread its waters over a space of ground nearly seven miles in circumference. When the waters extend so far as to obstruct the working of the mills at Helstone and Carminouse, the millers apply to Mr Rogers, as Lord of the Manor, and presenting him with two leathern purses, each containing three halfpence, solicit his permission to open the Bar. This being granted, workmen are employed by the Mayor of Helstone, to cut a passage through the pebbles; and the opening is no sooner made, than the whole body of water rushes through the aperture with wonderful force and impetuosity. Indeed the conflict between the wave and the river at these times constitutes an extraordinary spectacle, and this is often visible, six or eight miles from the shore; yet such is the peculiar situation of the place, and force of the rolling surge, that the bar of pebbles is formed again in a few days.

Dolly Pentreath

Before we quit this part of the Country, it may not be uninteresting to transcribe the account of Dolly Pentreath, who was born and buried in the village of Mousehole, not far from hence. This woman lived to the age of 102, and was one of the last persons who could speak the Cornish language. In the year 1768, she was visited by the Honourable Daines Barrington, whose report, that he had met with a woman in the County able to converse in this tongue not meeting with that degree of credit to which its accuracy was entitled occasioned him to make further inquiries concerning her, but this was not till several years afterwards, when he found, in 1773, that she was still living, and in tolerable health, though in her eighty seventh year. She was then "maintained by the Parish, and partly by fortune telling, and gabbling Cornish". In the former part of her life, she procured a maintenance by selling fish, and was well known in the Market of Penzance, where, at twelve years of age she sold her wares, conversing at that time in the langauage of her forefathers. In the year 1776, the same gentleman mentions her being still living, though exceedingly deaf. Her Epitaph is both in Cornish and English, and as the sentiment it expresses is somewhat whimsical, it is here inserted:

Coth Dol Pentreath canz ha Deaw
Mahir in Bedans en Powl pleu
Na en an Eglar ganna Poble braz
Bet en Eglar Hay Coth Dolly es!

Old Dolly Pentreath one hundred age and two,
Both born and in Paul Parish buried too,
Not in the Church, 'mongst people great and high,
But in the Church Yard doth Old Dolly lie.

Penrhyn

From Helston, we proceeded through Penrhyn to Falmouth, which is twelve miles distant. Penrhyn is a large town, pleasantly situated on the declivity of a hill, on the opposite side of the water to St Gluvias, in which Parish it is wholly included. Its present population is 2324.

Falmouth

We arrived at Falmouth at about four o'clock, and spent the Evening at Wynne's Hotel, where we met with the worst attention and the most direct incivility we had experienced on the road; and this I could not but attribute to their being used to company, who were waiting for Packets to Lisbon, or the West Indies, are obliged to put up with every inconvenience and imposition; but as I hear there is another Inn set up in opposition to Wynne's Hotel, I trust it will hereafter produce a good effect.

The Town is situated at the bottom of an eminence which commands the harbour. The houses are principally disposed in one street, nearly a mile in length, and running by the side of the beach. The quay is exceedingly convenient, as the water is of sufficient depth to admit vessels of considerable burthen to land their goods upon the warf. The harbour is capacious, and the convenience it affords to the shipping from the high lands that environ it, is equal to that obtained in any part of the kingdom. The Custom House, and Salt Office, for most of the Cornish Towns, are established at Falmouth. The inhabitants of this Parish, were enumerated under the late Act, at 1963 males, and 2886 females, inclusive of about 500 sailors and soldiers that usually reside here.

Tol men

From Falmouth, we rode to see a prodigious Druidical remain called Tol men, which stands on the top of a hill, and as at Carnbre is surrounded by immense fragments of rocks. This stone is supported on two smaller ones, and measures thirty three feet long, and fifteen high, supposed to weigh seven hundred and fifty tons. It is of an oval shape, and, I understand, at the top of it, is a large hole scooped into it, big enough to contain a man, which, they tell you was used by the Druids in delivering their oracles. I took two sketches of it, but the weather being unfavourable, we could see nothing of the view from it, though it stands on some of the highest ground in the County, and on a fine day, Plymouth, and the farthest extent of Cornwall are from thence visible.

Falmouth

November 15

We went on board a Dutch ship repairing upon the shore, eleven hundred tons burthen, one of the clumsiest I ever saw, and here Mr J. Flammank was seized with a nervous fit, and could not prevail on himself to venture down the rope ladder by which we ascended the deck, and it was with the greatest difficulty, partly by persuasion, partly by force, that I relieved him from his unpleasant situation. The principal Merchants of Falmouth are some Quakers of the name of Fox, I think Brothers of Dr Fox of Bristol. I was desirous of going on board a fine frigate lying off the harbour, which brought over the Ambassador from Portugal last Sunday, but could not accomplish it: she carries forty four guns, and some Sailors told me is by no means inferior to our ships of the same size.

French Prisoners

Mounting our horses at twelve, we proceeded on the road to Truro, but were detained upwards of an hour, just as we were leaving the Town by observing some French prisoners landed, they were two hundred and eighty in number, they were taken in two ships, the one a Corvette, and the other a Brig, by Sir Edward Pellew, the former of twenty four, and the latter of sixteen guns. I could not but remark, that the Officers had not the least aapearance of gentlemen, and several as if they had been mostly risen from before the mast.

The road between Falmouth and Truro, is in some places pretty, but wants trees and foliage. We arrived at Truro to a four o'clock dinner, and being much fatigued, went early to bed.

Truro

Truro is situated in a vale, at the conflux of two small rivers, the Kenwyn and St Allen, which direct their streams on each side of the town, and at the bottom unite with a branch of Falmouth harbour: at every Spring tide they form a fine Lake or body of water, two miles in length, and of sufficient depth to be navigable for vessels of one hundred tons. This advantage of situation, has doubtless been a principle cause of its rapid progress, and the preeminance it now enjoys amongst the Cornish towns.

Truro comprises three Parishes, St Mary, St Clement, Kenwyn. The Church is a spacious fabric, of that elegant kind of architecture, which flourished in England about the time of Henry the Seventh. It consists of two aisles of an equal size, and a smaller one; and has a modern steeple, of very inharmonious proportions, and by no means corresponded with the body of the church; which is very similar in its architecture to that of Launceston.

In the windows are several fragments of painted glass; and on one of them, on the South side, is the date 1518, the year when the Church was erected! On the North side of the Church, is a monument with the following inscription :

To the pious and well deserving memory of OWEN Fitz Pen. Phippe. who travelled overy many parts of the world, and on the 24th March 1620, was taken by the Turks, and made a captive in algier. He projected several plots for his liberty, and on the 17th of June 1627, with ten other Christian captives, Dutch and French, (persuaded by his counsel and courage) he began a cruel fight with 65 Turks, in their own ship, which lasted three hours, in which five of his companions were slain, yet God made him conquer, and so he brought the ship into Carthagena, being 400 ton and 22 ordce. The King sent for him to Madrid to see him, he was offered a Captain's place, and the King's favour, if he would turn Papist, which he refused. He sold all for £6000, returned into England and died at Lamoran, the 17th of March, 1636.

Truro

Melcombe in Dorset was the place of his birth,
Aged 54, and here lies earth to earth.

Truro
a Coinage town

Truro, as has been before mentioned is one of the original Coinage towns; and here only and at Penzance, with the exception of a few times at Helston, for the convenience of the merchants, have the Coinage of late years taken place. Most of the tin is coined here, and more is exported hence, than from any other port in the Country. The blocks lie in heaps about the streets, and are left unguarded, as their great weight renders it difficult to remove them without immediate detection. Here is a Coinage Hall; and Hals in his Parochial History, mentions, the town as possessing one, as early as the reign of King John. There is also a manufactory for converting block tin into bars and ingots: the weight of the former is from eight ounces to one pound; those of the latter from sixty to seventy pounds each. these bars are exported into the Mediterranean and Baltic; the ingots are sent to the East Indies. considerable quantities of Copper ore are dispatched from this town to Wales; in addition to the different branches of trade connected with the mines, a new source of business was established here, about ten years ago, by some tradesmen. This was a manufactory for carpets, which is now carried on with considerable success; over the Town Hall, and Market Place is this inscription.

T.B. Jenkin Daniel, Mayor
Who seeks to find eternal treasure
Must use no guile in weight or measure. 1615.

*Recent improvements
Truro*

The improvements made in Truro of late years, have been very considerable, and particularly since the passing the lighting and paying act, at Midsummer 1794. The principal street was formerly contracted, and disfigured by a row of houses, stretching along the middle from the Coinage Hall to the Market place. These have been removed, and a spacious opening formed, from which a new street is now building, diverging from the other at right angles, through which the road proceeds to Falmouth. the charges of paving, etc, are defrayed by a small assessment on each house. Among other objects which diversify the town, and reflect credit on its inhabitants, and the gentlemen of Cornwall, is a literary society and County Library established here in the year 1792. This was originally instituted, and is still patronised and supported by the Cornish Nobility and Gentry. A Theatre and Assembly room have been also erected in that part of the town called the High Cross; and on the 12th of August, 1799*, a County Infirmary was opened in Kenwyn Parish, under the patronage of the Prince of Wales. The expencesare defrayed by subscription; the regulations for the management of the sick, and for the active superintendance over the persons employed to attend them, are conceived with much judgement. The Infirmary is a new and spacious stone building.

*Local government of
Truro*

The government of Truro, is vested in a Mayor, four Aldermen, and twenty Capital Burgesses. The right of returning Members is vested in these twenty five persons only; though the number of inhabitants in the three parishes, as ascertained under the late Act, is 4542. The houses were enumerated at 775. The interest of the Borough since the exchange of Tregony with Lord de Dunstanville, has been wholly possessed

* The County Infirmary here opened in 1799 which postdates Skinner's tour.

by Lord Falmouth. On the election of a Mayor, the Town Mace by the custom of the Borough, must be delivered to the Lord of the Manor who retains it, till he is paid sixpence from every house as an acknowledgement.

Polgooth Mine

From Truro, we rode to a Mine called Polgooth, calling on my old friend Stackhouse in the way; he unfortunately was from home. We arrived at the Mine just at dinner time, and took our seats among twelve or fourteen Captains, as they are called, or in other words, Overseers of the workmen. The man who sat at the head of the table was a Quaker; and another, at my right hand, a Methodist; they, notwithstanding their differences in religious opinions, seemed to agree with each other perfectly well, and rivals only in who should eat the most.

Mining practice

The manner the Miners covenant for working, is I understand, by the job: a set of men, about eight or ten, bargain for a piece of ground for such a number of days, and agree to pay a portion of their gains to the Lord of the Manor; a quarter I believe, and on these conditions all the ore they raise belongs to themselves, till the term is expired: the proprietor then makes fresh conditions with them, according to the supposed value of their discoveries; sometimes they are unsuccessful, and perhaps work the whole time without gaining any thing; but at others they stand a chance of becoming quite rich. One of the Captains told me he had lately paid two men at the rate of eighty pounds per day, for ten days. They had agreed to try for ore on a piece of ground which they hired for two months; all but ten days of their time was expired before they discovered any thing, till all of a sudden, they found so rich a vein, they cleared the abovementioned sum. By these means, even the commonest labourer, has a chance of bettering his situation, should fortune favour him; and some of the first families in the County have risen to oppulence, by these means. We went all over the works of the Mine, but did not think it worthwhile to descend, it being late in the evening, and all the men were busy receiving their money: one of them I sketched in his mining dress, and the fellow seemed vastly pleased with the honour done him, but more so with the compensation he received. The account I have collected of these celebrated Mines is as follows:

Polgooth Mine described

Polgooth is particularly distinguished for its extensive, and rich tin works. The shafts by which the Miners descend, and through which the ore is raised to the surface, are scattered over a considerable extent of sterile ground, whose dreary appearance, and the sallow countenances of the Miners, concur to excite ideas of gloom, apprehension, and melancholy. The number of shafts are not less than fifty; from twenty to thirty of which are constantly in use. The descent into the Mine is by means of ladders, placed nearly perpendicularly: at the foot of each ladder is a narrow break, or landing place: and at certain intervals, are openings into different beds of ore. The main vein of ore is about six feet thick, runs from East to West, and dips to the North, at the rate of six feet in a fathom. Towards the East it divides into two branches; and there is another, that cuts the other nearly at a right angle, and consequently runs North and South, dipping to the East. The depth of the engine shaft is 124 fathoms, and the machine draws up a column of water at each stroke, 56 fathoms deep, and 15 inches in diameter. The ore is disseminated in general through a matrix of caple* accompanied with the yellow cupreous pyrites, and sometimes a ferruginous ochre. It is of the vitreous kind, but rarely found in crystals; the colour for the

---

* This probably refers to the Cornish word, more usually spelt capel, and refers to the mineral black tourmaline.

most part is greyish brown. The Country of the ore, is chiefly of a greyish killas.

About fifty or sixty feet below the surface of this Mine, the water that percolates through the different strata, begins to form small streams, which would soon increase, and overflow the lower part of the Mine, if not constantly conveyed away. The process is performed by the stupendous steam engine, noticed above, which raises the water to the adit level like the fountain of a river. The quantity of coals requisite to fill the fire place beneath the boilers of this immense machine is sixty bushels; and the consumption every twenty four hours, is about three weigh and a half; or 144 bushels. The expence of erecting an engine, is nearly £20,000. The whole operation of the machine may be suspended by a slight pressure on a sort of bolt attached to a large valve. Borlase mentions, that in his time the produce of this Mine was so great that the proprietors gained £20,000 annually, for several successive years. The revenues now gained from it are very large: but it has not always been so productive, as about the year 1754, it stopped working altogether, the receipts having exceeded the charges only ten pounds in the preceeding years! though the expenditure was at that time £100,000.

Dolcoath Mine, Camborne
This was the richest of the Cornish mines, and Polgooth
probably did not look so different in its heyday

St Austell

From the Mine we rode to St Austle, only a mile distant, where we took up our quarters for the night. This place has a Market, but is not a Borough Town, though of considerable more importance than many places that depute representatives in this County. It occupies the eastern side of a hill, which slopes gradually to a small rivulet that bubbles along a narrow valley. This stream, as well as the inequality of the ground has been rendered exceedingly useful to the tin manufacturers in the neighbourhood, as the water has been conducted round the side of the hills, and in its course, impells the machinery of several stamping mills which have been erected on different levels. It is also employed to cleanse and separate the tin from the founded matrix, by passing through several buddles.

This town, through its vicinity to the great Mine of Polgooth and some others, has within the last fifty years, considerably increased in the number of its houses and inhabitants. The holding of the Blackmore Court here, which is the most considerable of all the Stannary Courts, has also contributed to its increase and prosperity. The old town, or rather village, was at some little distance to the East; and its site is still marked by a few cottages. The present town had the turnpike carried through it, about thirty or forty years ago, and has since been a regular thoroughfare for travellers, from Plymouth to Land's End. The streets are very narrow, and not having any pavement for foot passengers, are somewhat unsafe.

Holy Trinity Church
St Austell

The Church is a handsome fabric, dedicated to St Austin*, consisting of three aisles. The Tower, and some of the other parts of the structure, are fancifully ornamented; various carvings, monstrous heads, angels, and other figures appear on the cornices.

* Holy Trinity Church, restored 1870.

St Austell
The tower of Holy Trinity Church here looms large

Round the second story of the Tower, are eighteen statues in rich ornamented niches; six on the West side, and four on each of the others. Those on the West are imagined to represent God the Father, with the crucified Saviour resting on his knees, below them are Joseph and Mary, and other figures. The remaining twelve, are supposed to be designed for the Apostles. On the South porch is an inscription in relief, on a stone one foot nine inches long, by one foot two inches. The first line appears to be the Cornish words, Ry Du, and to signify, God is a King; the second contains the initial letters of Jesus Nazarenus rex Judaeorum. Various other explications are however given to this inscription; and the best informed Antiquaries, seem undetermined as to the true meaning. The shields or ornaments on the outside of this fabric, are also carved on many of the seats; and from the repetition of the shovel, pick axe, and hammers, and other tools, it seems probable that the Miners were the principal contributors towards the expences of the building.

The inhabitants of the town are chiefly employed in the pilchard fishery, in mining, and in a small manufactory of coarse woollens, and their population returned under the late act, amounts to 3888, of those 1994 are males, and 1874 females; the houses are 707.

Blowing Houses

At the West end of this town are the only Blowing Houses in Cornwall. these are three in number, and very spacious. In two of them Cylinders are employed instead of bellows; and this mode of fluxing the ore, is considered by the workmen as far preferable to the other. The old smelting houses are supplied with coals, and are reverberatory; but in these blowing houses, the fire is made of charcoal, and ignited by air impelled through tubes by the cylinders.

The farms in the Parish are in general small, none of them exceed £150 per annum; but the ground near the town, is chiefly let in separate fields, which are rented at a very high rate, varying from three to five pounds an acre. From the increase of inhabitants, the value of land has been doubled within these last ten years. The great tythes are the inheritance of Lord Camelford and Mr Tremayne, they are rented by Mr Charles Rash-leigh. The usual composition is; six shillings an acre for wheat, and four shillings for oats. The small tythes belong to the Vicar, who has always been contented with the small sum of ninepence in the pound. The value of a lease for three lives, is here estimated at sixteen years gross rent. The average duration of these kind of leases in Cornwall, is about thirty years.

Porthmear

We left St Austle about ten, and in our way back to Bodmin, visited a little fishing place called Porthmear, or Charles Town*, which is situated on the North side of St Austle Bay. Its whole importance if not its entire origin, is to be attributed to the spirited and merito-rious exertions of the above mentioned Charles Rash-liegh, Esq., under whose vivifying patronage, from a poor Hamlet, too contemptible for description, it has become in a very few years, a place of considerable magnitude, and is still increasing, both in extent and consequence.

China clay

The chief article of commerce from Porthmear, is St Stephen's China Stone, whose properties were first observed by a Quaker named Cookworthy. This gent-leman was present at the founding of some bells at Fowey, and from observing the appearance of some of the stone which had been contained in the mould, was induced to commence a manufactory at Plymouth, but failed soon afterwards. A second attempt was made at Bristol, but proved equally unsuccessful. The late Josiah Wedgewood, then took a tract of ground in

---

* Work on a granite harbour and dock at Charlestown, the called West Porthmear, was begun in 1791 and a small Georg. township remains almost unspoilt.

which the china stone was found, and by his superior skill, employed it with complete success. Upwards of sixty carts are now employed in the carriage of the stone from the quarry to the harbour of Charlestown.

To the eye of the Antiquary are greater attractions, for on the downs between Porthmear and St Austle, there are still remaining nearly twenty round Barrows, several of which are in a line, and not far distant from each other. These probably are of British origin, as in making the new road between the above places, some of them were cut through, and several of the British instruments found which are at present at Manabilly. Near them is a large unhewn stone, standing upright, and about fourteen feet in height; and about three or four miles further, by the side of the road, I took a sketch of a Cottage, in which was born the great Mr Allen of Prior Park. It is on an estate belonging to Mr Caer Lyon of Tregrean in the Parish of St Blaizey. The house has nothing in appearance to recommend it beyond other cottages, but curiosity impelled me to secure a remembrance of it, as a lesson for industry, since this truly great man, without friends or interest, or even education, beyond that of a common school, was able to push his fortune in the world, and secure the friendship of the great, not less on account of his liberality and public spirit, than for his judgement, clear reasoning, and polite conversation. The drawing of this cottage, I mean as a companion to one of Prior Park, and one glance of the eye, will convey this useful moral, never to distrust ourselves, for by the assistance of Providence, and our own unremitting attention, much may be done, although fortune may at first seem to oppose us. The country, as we passed some miles beyond, afforded some interesting views, one of which I endeavoured to take of a rockly cliff in the parish of Llanlivery, which is certainly very picturesque. Leaving

Ralph Allen

Lostwithiel to the right, we arrived at Bodmin to dinner, having in the eigh days we were absent, ridden 161 miles, besides walking; and I must confess I felt somewhat fatigued; however the Doctor having engaged me to a party I was under the necessity of dining out, and did not get to bed till past midnight.

November 18

It being a rainy morning, I staid within doors till one o'clock, when I went in company of Mr Fisher, of Pembroke College, Oxford, to sketch a view on the river Camel, which indeed I think will form one of the prettiest pictures I have taken on my tour. We returned home to dinner a little after three.

November 19

I read prayers and preached for the Doctor at Llanhydrock, and in the Evening performed duty at Bodmin Church.

November 20

It being rainy, I was confined within doors the whole morning. Dined with a Mr Wallace, where I met Newman an old College acquaintance, now a Captain in the Somerset Militia.

November 21

I took with the Doctor his usual walk to Boscarn; and it being agreed that we should set out Eastwards the morning after, we sent our horses forward to Oakhampton, by his servant: I dined and supped at home, with the Doctor and his family.

November 22

After a great deal of bustle on the part of the Doctor, who was out of bed as soon as it was light, we made shift to get into a Post chaise a little after eleven, and without seeing anything of notice, arrived to dinner at Launceston, where I met with a good French engraving of Voltaire, which I purchased of the Innkeeper for seven shillings and sixpence. We arrived at Oakhampton at half past nine, though not without a thousand fears, on the part of my nervous companion, who wished to get out of the Chaise and walk down every hill, which I successfully opposed, it not only being dark, but a very stormy night, which would not have rendered the opening of the carriage door every half mile every agreeable.

November 23

The Doctor having business on the road to detain him, I proceeded alone on horseback, and slept at Exeter.

November 24

I slept at Bridgewater.

November 25

The Doctor arrived late on the last evening at the Inn: during supper, I made him promise to be in Wells, by two o'clock this day, that we might arrive at Claverton together, although we had travelled so much asunder. I breakfasted at Piper's Inn, and got to Wells at twelve, and saw my Brother William, who eat a beef

Wells

Claverton

steak with me, and the Doctor not coming accompanied me five miles on my road. About half past four, it began to rain most violently, so that I reached Claverton in an hour after, almost in the same plight I did Old Down Inn, the day I quitted home, being wet to the skin. The Doctor I afterwards heard was seized with the gout on the twenty fifth, which confined him at Wells, so that I was kept in a state of anxiety till he arrived at Claverton two days afterwards.

A list of the miles, stages, and Inns, from Claverton:

	miles	
From Claverton to Wells is	22	The Swan
Wells to Piper's Inn	10	
Piper's Inn to Bridgewater	11	The George
Bridgewater to Taunton	12	The Castle
Taunton to Cullumpton	19	The Half Moon
Cullumpton to Exeter	12	New London
Exeter to Oakhampton	22	White Hart
Oakhampton to Launceston	20	White Hart
Launceston to Bodmin	21	
	149	
Bodmin to Sidmouth and back	30	179

Western Tour

First Day	From Bodmin to St Michael's	15	
	St Michael's to Redruth	16	
	Redruth to Cambron	4	
			35
Second Day	Cambron to Schaddy Park	3	
	Schaddy Park to Hale	8	
	Hale to Marazion	6	
	Marazion to Penzance	3	
			20
Third Day	Penzance to St Just	10	
	St Just to Land's End	6	
	Land's End to Logan Stone	5	
	Logan Stone to Penzance	10	
			31
Fourth Day	Penzance to Helston		14
Fifth Day	Helston to Falmouth	12	
	Going to and returning from Tolmen	3	
			15
Sixth Day	Falmouth to Truro	12	
Seventh Day	Truro to St Austle	14	
Eighth Day	St Austle to Bodmin	14	
			155
	Returning from Bodmin	149	
	Going to Bodmin and Western Tour	334	
		483	

Besides riding on an average daily 10 Miles

THE WALKER'S COMPANION

A Collection for all who enjoy the countryside on foot

The works of some 23 writers, beginning with Wordsworth and ending with Henry Williamson are quoted here and all illustrate some aspect of the walker's art. The urge to get away from it all and get close to nature opens us to the varied pleasures of walking: the pursuit of health, relaxation and renewal. All these are celebrated in prose and poetry. So too are the delights of the country footpath and mountain track, whether they be the fruits of a day's ramble or of an extended walking tour.

The West of England figures prominently in this anthology, in particular Wilkie Collins' hiking through Cornwall and excerpts from two accounts of marathon walks undertaken in the last century: Walter White from London to Land's End in 1854 and the American Elihu Burritt walking between the same two points ten years later. The former trekked 425 miles during the month of August on a budget of £10. Both accounts are full of interest and some of the most entertaining and illuminating incidents are quoted in this absorbing collection.

This remarkable collection of prose and verse . . . a charming ramble of a book
Wiltshire Gazette and Herald

Illustrated with pen and ink sketches by Edward Dowden
A5 Paperback   112 pages   Price £2.95

Available from bookshops or post free from the publishers:
Ex Libris Press, 1 The Shambles, Bradford-on-Avon, Wiltshire